Blooms

Out of Trials

and Tribulations

Also by Margaret Santos

Blooms

Out of Trials

and Tribulations

Margaret Santos

vase on Table Publishing

Author: Margaret Santos.
Mississauga, Ontario, Canada
E-mail: margaretsantos31@gmail.com

Title: *Blooms: Out of Trials and Tribulations*
ISBN: 978-1-9992892-6-3
Category: Books-Literature & Fiction-Poetry-Women Authors

Book Cover Image: pixabay.com: KIMDAEJEUNG
Vector Image: pixabay.com: Gordon Johnson
              OpenClipart-Vectors from Pixabay

Publisher: Vase On Table Publishing
Toronto, Canada
Contact: +1 647 299-6181

Dedication

All those people who wanted to make a significant change in their own lives and in the lives of those around them.

Contents

Introduction

Blooms is a collection of poems that I have written over the past decade or so. It is also a book for adults as it contains some mature subject matter that wouldn't be appropriate for children.

The poems in this book are some of the best works I've ever done. These poems are special to me because of the emotions I have when I read them. Some of the poetry in this book reminds me just how lucky I am to be alive. While others remind me of some of the people who I have been so blessed and so privileged to be able to call my friends. Some of them have gone on to better and brighter things, yet others have passed away, and are no longer with us, but as I explained before, dying is just another part of living. It's the circle of life. There's a beginning - your birth, a middle - your life and an end - your death.

Some of these poems will make me cry every time I read them. I feel strong emotions when I read the poems or even the topic of a poem. Sometimes when I think of the person or group of people that the poems are about, I smile or shed tears of both joy and sadness. That's the great thing about poetry, you could put a whole bunch of words together and it doesn't matter who is reading them, different people will have different reactions, emotions, as well as messages to take away from each poem.

I write poetry because it is a creative way to express myself and deal with subject matters that are important to me. Such subject matters include feminism, mental health issues, ableism, mothers and fathers and how children could be raised to grow into productive caring, compassionate, kind, loving empathic members of society. I have poetry about friends, and the way they have influenced me over the years. Some of my poems are on gratitude, love, volunteering and on some of the things that have affected me both positively and negatively, and the different coping strategies - some successful, some not - which I've used.

I hope my book, *Blooms*, inspire you to leave a lasting and positive impression on others and if you are feeling discouraged and beaten down, may it restore your spirit and reinvigorate you. It is my deepest desire that you will read my poems and find the fortitude to soar above your darkest days if you have any. And if not, may you find fresh motivation to keep on making this world a better place. If you have left a positive impact on this world, then in my opinion, you have fulfilled your purpose as a human being.

Hidden Self

*I put up these invisible walls so no one will see
the real true me.
Invisibility, now that is the key.
I keep people at arm's length
For instance.
Please don't stand too close to me,
for I really do value my personal space.
I may laugh or smile when least expected
I can not help it.
Sometimes, I cannot feel the muscles in my face.
I tend to push people away when I am not feeling safe and secure.
When I am feeling uncertain of myself and unsure.
When I am feeling hurt, lonely, and ridiculed
I tend to wear my emotions on my sleeve.
That is an oxymoron if I have ever heard one.
I want to be heard and not seen
From fear of being laughed at or mocked.
Being alone for long was never my strong suit.
But please do not stand too close to me.
I really do value my personal space. You may like to dispute,
That a person who chooses to be heard and not seen likes to be alone;
However, I need connection in my life every now and again.
I think the key to feeling whole and complete.
Is loving yourself unconditionally.
I need to feel loved, accepted, and appreciated for all of me.
Just the way I am with all my strengths and flaws and insecurities.
I need to be able to express myself without fear of judgement.
From fear of being ridiculed
I think what it all comes down to*

is not caring what others think and do.
Do not worry you can make it through,
Just by being true to yourself,
and ultimately being your very best you.

The Story Behind Hidden Self

At first, I was trying to hide my true identity from those around me, my family, my friends, and my acquaintances. I think it was because I was hurt so bad in the past, physically, emotionally, sexually, psychologically, as well as financially. I was inadvertently taught to be seen and not heard. That is why I hesitate to let people get too close to me. I have allowed people to get close to me in the past, but then I got burned. So, hence the reason for not really trusting anyone and letting anyone get too close to me; also all my secrets are tightly guarded.

There are two points in my life when I have totally let my guard down; the first time wasn't entirely my choice. I was vulnerable due to my inability to walk independently and the weight I had lost. I think due to the mental health problems that I was struggling with at the time because of all I had gone through at home and school, I was in a bad way, but somehow I managed to get through it. Whether it be to my mother's persistence at me having to call her every hour on the hour. Or whether it was my will to live, I'm not sure. Finally, I managed to turn things around for myself when I had to have a bilateral hip transplant on a count of all the trauma my body had endured; at least, that's what I believe, anyway. It was a lot of hard work, and some tears were shed by both my mother and me.

The second time I had this Ah-ha moment was when I got confused about what a team member had done to me and what my brother had done to me. That is when I sought help from a psychologist, and I sorted out what had actually happened to me versus what were just triggers for me. I also learned to have so much more compassion for myself and others. I would say it has really helped me to heal myself a lot. I am at the point now where I can say I am truly happy and content with every aspect of my life.

I had to learn to love myself first with all of my strengths, flaws, and insecurities. I had to do a lot of praying. I had to do a lot of soul-searching. I learned how to take care of myself and love myself unconditionally. I still continue to work on some things with the help of my doctor and the psychologist.

Friendship

I have met some really great friends along the way
Some friends will last a life time.
Why can't some of them choose to stay?
Some of them will choose to be forever, mine.
Some will make you feel great by just giving you a great big smile.
Some friends have the ability to make you laugh by all the silly
things they do.
Some will take the time for you to walk that extra smile.
Those who are your true friends, would do anything for you.
No matter the time of day, no matter the circumstance
That's what friends are for, right?
If you make mistakes, that's okay because they would give you a
second chance.
Friends can also make you quite bright.
Friends do things out of the goodness of their heart,
Without expecting anything in return they could help you to make a
brand-new start.
Friends are patient and kind with ones hopes and dreams,
Friends do not need to boast or need to be jealous.
And they are understanding of another person's needs.
Friends are a gift sent from heaven up above, actually quite precious.
Friends are not rude or egotistical.
They do not insist on getting their own way.
Some friends can be quite responsible and ethical.
They just take it day by day.
Friends are not irritable or resentful, they just seek the truth.
Friends do not try to find ways to get others in trouble.
They might even share their favourite chocolate bar with you, like a
Baby Ruth.

Blooms

Friends can also be quite remarkable.
Those who you hold nearest and dearest will always love you no matter what you do.
That is why they are your friend's true blue.

The Story Behind Friendship

My poem on friendship reflects what some of my friends meant to me over the years, the characteristics of some of my friends, as well as what it means to have my friend's best interest at heart.

I met some of my friends where I currently reside. I have friends who are residents and others who are team members. I have friends I have kept in touch with over many years. We still meet up for coffee tea and birthdays. People who have been my friends for a short while are as important to me as those who have been my friends for a really long time.

The lessons friends have taught me have played a significant role in my development. For instance, some of my friends have taught me the gift of letting people help me. Some have taught me the trait of humility. In other words, I need to start thinking of myself less, and begin thinking of others first and foremost. Characteristics that my friends have are humility, kindness, a forgiving spirit, a loving and caring heart and open-mindedness. They are compassionate, patient, understanding, and intelligent.

The way I tend to take care of my friends is by asking them how they're doing and I try to make them laugh when they are feeling sad. I listen attentively to their problems and offer some of my resources when and where I feel they will be useful. Friends will come and go, but if you have fond memories then that will last you a life-time.

"Some of my friends have passed away, and others have moved on to better and brighter things." While others have moved on to further their career or left due to marriages, differences in opinions of the way things are done here, or whatever the reason may be. There are always going to be those friends who you will be able to count on no matter what and others that aren't going to be there for you. And what I would say to that is you cherish them while they're in your life and when they are gone you wish them well, and send them some love and light. Upon the passing of some of my dearest friends I have learned the art of letting go; I have also learned that unfortunately dying is a part of life. You're born. You live. You die. That's it.

Journey

Thank you for always believing in me.
Thank you for looking for potential, where we just could not see.
I think it is our purpose to discover who we truly are.
Thank you for accompanying us on this journey.

Thank you for helping us along the way this far.
Thank you for being like a shining star.
You have helped us throughout the years to get dressed, and to feel all better.
Thank you for raising the bar.

When we were feeling cold or under the weather;
you would go and get us a blanket or a sweater.
When we were feeling sad, lonely, or blue;
you made us feel like we truly mattered.
If we ever felt bored or didn't know what to do; you would provide entertainment.
Thank you for lifting our spirits higher and higher.

Thank you for always encouraging us to try new things and to attend different events.
Thank you for the time together we spent.
Thank you for helping us spiritually.
Thank you for what you have meant

Thank you for caring for us so abundantly.
Thank you for putting things so simply.
Thank you for trying to teach us tolerance in your own special way.
Thank you for helping us ever so gently.

Thank you for teaching us patience day by day.
Thank you for listening to what we have to say.
Here are to our forever friends.

Margaret Santos

We want to stay.
As we climb one step closer up that ladder to heaven;
to our journeys end.
Here are to our forever friends.

The Story Behind Journey

The poem "Journey" is a love letter to the Team that has worked here over the years. It is a heart-felt expression of gratitude for what they have done for me and the residents living in this facility called The Village of Erin Meadows, where I have lived for the past ten years. For the most part, those years have been happy ones.

The nurses keep us healthy, working long hours to see we have our medication and, if needs be, acting quickly to deal with any emergencies.

The recreation therapists keep us busy and entertained, so we never get bored. They engage us in art programs, baking, entertainment, exercise and all kinds of activities.

The pastor cares for all our spiritual needs and can assist with end-of-life practices.

Housekeeping keeps the place spotless, cleaning the floors, hallways and bathrooms.

Personal support workers help to take care of our personal hygiene. They comb our hair, brush our teeth, or help us to the bathroom if we need assistance.

There is also the kinesiologist and the physiotherapist who care for our physical well-being by providing various exercises, some of which we can do by ourselves, while we may need assistance with others.

Then there is the leadership team who help to keep everything running smoothly or to the best of their ability anyways.

When all is said and done, we are basically a happy bunch.

Margaret Santos

My Tattoo

At first it was hard to decide.
Whether or not to get one
After all was said and done
It was my decision,
And I would have to live with this very permanent image on my
body.
So, after a lot of contemplation
I, finally decided to get a tattoo.
The question was what would be an image or words which I could
live with permanently.
When I got older and my skin would start to wrinkle
What could I live with and be truly happy?
Well, at first, I thought about words that had special meaning to me.
But then I thought nah! I don't want people reading stuff on me.
I want it to have special meaning
But I'm the only one who'd know what it meant.
If people ask then I would do my best to try and explain it to them.
Now, the funny part is I hadn't decided until about a month before.
I went to go and get it done.
I'm not going to lie to you, it was expensive.
I actually broke the bank to get it done.
Not a wise move on my part, but I did it just the same,
Then to my utter surprise there on my upper left shoulder blade
there they were the yin/yang symbol and a butterfly on a flower.
No, I did not get a chance to look at it
She took a picture and showed me.
Something about having it mysteriously hidden away,
Me being the only one that knows where it is, it seems very exciting
to me.

Blooms

It hurt a little, not a lot.
The tattoo artist said, "Relax and take deep breaths!
You might even start to enjoy it."
Yeah right! Says the lady holding the needle in her hand
I didn't even cry,

Nope, not even one tear was shed.
Though, I wanted it to try
And I must admit it looks pretty spectacular, on my body.
Now, I want you to understand the reason why I got it done.
I think at the very moment she said, "Okay I'm done."
I felt like I had won the victory.
I had conquered all my fears at that very moment.
I got the tattoo of the butterfly to remind myself just how far I've
come in my journey.
The yin yang symbol to remind myself to live a life with balance,
And also, to remind myself that in each of us there is always the
possibility to do good or bad.
We must always try to remember to lean towards the good.
Now, that's the real reason behind my tattoo.

The Story Behind My Tattoo

I was 36 years young and I wanted to do something that would make me feel strong and independent. I had asked my shoulder surgeon if he saw any problems with me having a tattoo and this was about a year after I had had my partial left shoulder replacement. He said, "No," he didn't. So, then it was a matter of figuring out how I was going to get there safely, and who was going to go with me. Oh, yeah! and how much money it was going to cost me, and would I be able to afford it. That was my main concern, and finding a female tattoo artist. So, when I had figured all of that out and I was sure who was going to go with me I booked my ride there with Transhelp and me and my Recreation Therapist extraordinaire, Helen JY Choi, went with me on her day off mind you which was super sweet of her to give up her day off for me.

I don't know how many people have gotten tattoos but my shower day was the following day and I was not supposed to have a shower. I think as a way to cope I was just chatting away to the tattoo artist about different things, and at one point she said to me, "would you like me to continue, or should I stop what I'm doing?" I replied, "no you could continue" I think she was getting kind of frustrated with me as she was trying to concentrate and I was just chatting away trying to stay calm and relaxed.

I made it through and she got the job done, and as I said in my poem it looks freaking spectacular on my left shoulder blade. After it was all said and done, I did feel independent and stronger for having it done. When I did finally start to show it to people some were in shock, some asked did it hurt, others were appalled that I would do something like that to myself. In the end, it was my decision and I'm going to be the one who has to live with this very permanent image on my body and you know what I'm okay with that.

Volunteers

Volunteers are important to us
because it allows us to lend a helping hand.
It doesn't matter whether you are young or old.
It gives us the opportunity to take a stand.
It gives us the chance to do our best, and to be bold.
It gives you a chance to be a team player.
It gives you the opportunity to explore some
of the things you like and some of the things you don't.
It might also teach you to be more spiritual,
and to say your prayers.
It gives you the chance to figure out some
things you will do and some of the things you won't.
It gives you the chance to do as your told
and teaches you to follow instructions.
A person who performs a task willingly without pay.
A person who gets to choose his or her own options.
A person who volunteers with young children
or the elderly learns to take things day by day.
A person who offers freely to take part in a business.
Out of the goodness of their own heart.
Can choose to make a brand-new start.

The Story Behind Volunteers

The story behind this poem is about volunteers and the importance of getting that work experience without being paid. It can give a person the chance to discover what they want to do for an occupation. Or maybe it could give someone an opportunity to get to know a group of people that they are interested in working with as a career.

It also gives people the chance to lend a helping hand. It teaches people especially those who are young to follow instructions very carefully. It can also give people a chance to practice patience, active listening skills, compassion, empathy, using I statements to take ownership of one's own feelings or circumstances.

It does not matter how young or old you are, you can volunteer at any age. One can have the desire to help as young as five years old. If the desire to help is there, then the sky is the limit. It can also give you the possibility of finding somewhere to belong, to be a team player. It gives one the likelihood of developing some new skills that they never knew they had.

Ode to Julia!

She was such a small person, with such a huge personality
In such a confined place, she occupied a wide variety of space
Going here and there
In her motorized electric wheelchair
She was patient and kind
With a really strong mind
She was understanding and caring
She was also a great source of comic relief
She had a great sense of humour
She also loved flowers
Julia Morrison was one of a kind
She was a diva in her own special way
She had her own personal style, a fashionista you might say
She loved to people watch
Observing was her thing
You always knew when she was in the building
and when she had gone out
She was a part of the war, WWI or WWII
I'm not sure in which one she served
She had a heart and a spirit that just would not quit
I'm glad God put her on this earth,
But I know she is one of Gods angels watching over us
from heaven above
I think what I will miss about her most of all is how much joy she
spread
I'm glad her final moments were at home with us she spent
I'm glad God put her on this earth for us to love
For I know she is one of Gods angels watching over us from
heaven up above
She is in our hearts and we in hers and that is where she will
stay for all of eternity.

The Story Behind Ode to Julia!

This poem is about a dear friend of mine who we lost much too soon Mrs. Julia Morrison. She was such a treasure! Yes, she had her bad days, but I cannot recall a day when she was ever mean to me. She was such a small person with a huge personality. I remember I used to read a lot. I more often than not had a book in the basket of my walker, and one day I was sitting in the green house reading and she came up to me and said, "Margaret you never have to worry about feeling lonely as you've always got a friend in your books!" Now, that may sound lonely or pathetic to some people but I finally understand what she meant all those years ago, she meant that a really good book can take you to new places you've never been before.

Julia was an amazing friend, too! She had quite the presence about her. You always knew when she went out to the mall or to dialysis, as she was not well. She was always thinking of others, even those she didn't get along with very well. She made room in her heart for them. I can recall many a time we were playing Bingo on the Main Street and someone would want to sit at a table that was full and often times Julia would give up her spot to give someone else an opportunity to play, and she would go to the green house to hang out with her best pal Nancy.

We had a memorial service for her right here, The Village of Erin Meadows, where she took her last breath. Her family came to the service. If I am not mistaken, I think the poem on the previous page was read, by our dear friend Nancy McPhee.

True Friend, Dorothy Boorman
(May 27th, 1920 - January 1st, 2016)

*Dorothy was my friend
We had been through so much together
We stayed together through thick and thin
We were friends to the bitter end.
She will be my friend `till the end of time.
That`s what makes her forever mine
Her memory will live on for a very long time in my heart.
I shall miss her even in heaven.
She would`ve been ninety-seven this year.
Her husband went up to heaven on his own.
Leaving her to roam this earthly life all alone.
Now, I understand why she had to leave so soon.
She could still walk and talk
In fact, she would spend one third of her day on the exercise
bike in the fitness room.
She liked to stay physically fit, I think that was the secret to
her longevity.
She was so full of life.
Free of worry and of strife.
She was actually married to her husband Arthur for seventy years.
Mind you neither one of them could hear.
But now I could just imagine them up in heaven holding hands.
Dancing to all the music of the big bands.
She had interesting ways of doing things*

*She loved her coffee that was for sure.
She always said she had cancer of the throat and a funny mouth.
She was patient and kind.*

Margaret Santos

She liked to do word finds.
She also had a razor-sharp mind.
She was very religious.
She was also quite curious.
A bit on the busy side one might say.
Just taking it day by day.
Always walking, never stopping to sit for too long.
Her motto was if you don`t use it, you lose it.
And that is what she did until the bitter end.
She was the source of my inspiration.
That is why she remains to be to this very day, my forever friend.

The Story Behind True Friend, Dorothy Boorman
(May 27th, 1920 - January 1st, 2016)

Dorothy Boorman was another dear friend of mine who passed quite a while ago. She was from England or what one might call United Kingdom now. Oh, and she always used to have those peppermint candies in her purse. She would share them with me some of the time.

She often helped me to put on my clothes protector as she knew I wasn't capable of putting it on myself. She liked to keep busy, always doing her word finds or busy walking here and there, and of course working out on the exercise bike in the fitness room.

She was a great source of inspiration for me as she was always so independent even until the end. She always was very physically fit, and I think her motto was if you don't use it, you lose it.

Arthur and Dorothy were really close; they were always calling each other "Dear one," and she was always instructing him to exercise, and eat properly as I think he was diabetic. She was really close with one of our recreation therapists too, John Knox.

She was a sweet little old English lady except when she was angry with you. I remember this one time I gave her a Christmas present and she got so angry with me I think she nearly threw the present at me. At least, she yelled at me I remember that much, but after that we exchanged Christmas presents with each other right up until her final breath.

Margaret Santos

My Disability Does Not Define Me

My disability does not define me
I have Morquio Syndrome "B"
Or Muccopolysaccharidosis Type IV
You could say it is rare, that would be an understatement
To put it quite simply, it is a genetic disease that mainly affects my
joints and my movements
That`s why it is hard for me to walk
Oh, yes it affects my speech too, which makes it difficult to talk
Yet, it does not affect my ability to think or remember things
I can think quite clearly
I am short in stature
I am very mature
Sometimes a bit too serious, one might say, but I just take it day by
day
You see the last half of that word is ability, and that is what I try to
focus on
Otherwise, I may as well be dead and gone

I try to stay both mentally and physically strong.
There is so much that I can do
I can walk with the use of a walker
I hardly ever need to see the doctor
I can speak with the use of my communication device
I am as healthy as a horse
I have clean skin and clear pores

I am intelligent and kind,
I am beautiful from the inside out
Sometimes I do shout,
But that is only because I get so frustrated
Because my speech is limited,

Blooms

And people don't always take the time to understand
I am patient and caring
I am honest and quite daring
I have a great sense of humour
I am honourable, sensible, capable and quite responsible
I am also quite independent
I can write really well.

I would also like to increase my confidence
I am bright, and that`s really swell
So, you see, having a disability is not a hindrance, but it can increase
one's sense of perseverance
I can do everything a person living without a disability can do, only
at a much slower rate
So, if I am slow and make mistakes
Please. . . forgive me, for I am only human, and I was a gift sent
from God, so that must mean I am pretty special.

The Story Behind My Disability Does Not Define Me

I've got Morquio Syndrome Type B, and it is a genetic condition passed down from both my parents. Which means that both of my parents were carriers of this condition that I am currently living with, and will continue live with until the day I die. So, the just of it is I am missing the gene to break down these long chains of sugar molecules that build up in me, and it creates all these problems for my walking, my fine motor skills, my large motor skills, my neck, my back, and it affects all of my movements. My body is also riddled with rheumatoid arthritis.

The story behind the previous poem is explaining all about a person living with a disability, and how just because some of us may appear to be helpless, or just because our legs don`t work it does not mean that we are incompetent. For example, I went to the hairdresser`s recently and the lady who was cutting my hair asked what`s wrong with her, to the rec therapist who was with me. That`s what I`m saying we as humans form these silly preconceived assumptions about people all the time, without even giving people the benefit of the doubt to prove that we actually aren't just another pretty face, or whatever assumption they may have assumed about us.

So, to put things into perspective for anybody out there who may or may not have any preconceived notions of what living with a disability is like. It is just like living without one except for the fact that one might have to find different ways of doing things. I think what people need to focus on is the last half of that word which is "ability". So, what we need to start focusing on is what it is we can do and stop focusing on what it is we can`t do. That sounds much more helpful to me.

Do You Have Joy in your Feet?

Do You Have Joy in your Feet?
Do you have joy in your feet?
Like for instance, when you walk.
Do you strut? Like John Travolta in that movie?
Oh, what's it called, Saturday Night Fever?
Do you have joy in your feet?

Or do you walk like June Clever?
As in on that show 'Leave It To Beaver'.
Do you march, like a tin soldier?

Or do you hop, skip, or jump?
Do you have joy in your feet

Like a woman running to meet her child.
After he or she had been lost for a really long time.

It just might make you smile.
When you see two children playing?
It might be all worthwhile.
Do you have joy in your feet?

Like lots of new and interesting people you meet.
Like a chewy chocolate chip cookie.
That you eat.
Or like a person who just got promoted at work.
Do you have joy in your feet?

When you've got the opportunity to lend a helping hand?

And you can make someone's life better
When you keep those dearest to you around?
And you have both your feet firmly planted on solid ground.
Do you have joy in your feet?

When you've found inspiration and purpose for your life?
And you finally have got a goal.
And know in what direction your life is headed.
You can feel quite contented.
Do you have joy in your feet?

Now, can you walk as if your life is a dance.
You can begin to take a chance.
And have a new lease on life.
You can take a leap of faith, and take big, long strides.

Do you have joy in your feet?
Yes, I do.
And you know what? You can too

The Story Behind Do You Have Joy in your Feet?

The story behind "Do You Have Joy in your Feet?" is the connection between a person's walk and the way they're feeling. So, if a person struts like John Travolta in Saturday Night Fever that means that they must be feeling pretty confident and good about themselves.

Now, if one is walking like June Cleaver from that show called Leave it to Beaver than one might believe that person is in a pretty good mood too! However, if a person starts marching like a tin soldier, then someone may come to the conclusion that this person is angry or upset about something.

I am examining all of the instances where you might be walking differently depending on how you're feeling. If you are feeling tired, then you might be dragging your feet a little more had you not been feeling tired either physically or mentally. For example, when you have just found out that you got promoted at work, you've found inspiration or a goal you're particularly excited about that's why I ask "Do you have joy in your feet?"

I took this question from another poem I read called "Phenomenal Woman" by the late Maya Angelou, and I turned it into a poem of my own. Pretty clever eh! It makes me feel good about myself knowing that I could take a line from another poem from an author I admire so much.

A Celebration of Women

International Women`s Day is celebrated on March 8th
It is a chance for us to celebrate just how far we have come
here in North America, but
It is also a chance to fight for those girls and women less
fortunate than ourselves.
Those young girls who don't have opportunities like we do,
Such as, the chance to go to school.
The chance to vote, or to make oneself heard
The chance to have a voice
To have the audacity to make some noise,
The opportunity to make a choice.
To be loud, and to be proud
It gives us the chance as women to recognize how we are:
Such powerful and phenomenal individuals
How each of us were so masterfully created by a loving
and all-encompassing God.
How each of us can be so different yet be so similar
We are good listeners
We are all connected each of us to one another
We are all sisters
Whether we are related by blood or not.

We are looking for equal rights amongst men and women
Here in North America, we are looking for universal childcare
We are looking for women not to find themselves in such a
state of lonely solitaire.
We are also looking for a way to end violence against women
That is why we need men to get involved too.
We need equal rights for all ethnic backgrounds,

Blooms

For those of us who are poor, weak, and strong.
For each of us who possess wisdom and courage.
We need to stand up for those persons living with disabilities.
For those of us who are not strong enough to fight the battle,
yet want to win the war.
Against all odds and inequities.
As women we are looking for equal rights for all.
So, we can live peacefully and happily after all.

The Story Behind A Celebration of Women

A celebration of women is just what it says it's about a celebration of women. It's a chance to celebrate all women of different abilities, and of all different ethnicities.

It's a chance to fight for those women without as many rights as we have here in North America. It's about fighting for all women; those who are poor, weak, and struggling also, it's about standing up for those women living with disabilities.

The purpose of March 8th, is to celebrate all women and to recognize just how far we have come as a gender of people who were once not allowed to own property, to have a bank account, to vote, or even considered persons under the law. All the rights we have as well as, all the rights we still have to work towards. For example, affordable daycare, ending sexual assault, and domestic violence against women, ending violence against African Canadians and Indigenous women. The fact is we need to create opportunities for those women without equal pay. We also need to do something about body shaming in the current society that we live in.

As much as we need the women, we need the men too, to support us and to stand with us against all the injustices in the world.

What we are striving for is an egalitarian society, where we have equal opportunities for both men and women, and when we have created such a community of equal opportunities for all, then that is only when we could all be truly happy.

If I Were a Mother. . .

If I were a mother.....
I would be a great teacher
I would help my children with their homework.
I would teach them right from wrong.
I would help them to be courageous, kind, caring, intelligent
individuals who are strong.
I would teach them that it pays to do a little hard work.

I would be a good counsellor
I would offer my children guidance.
I would help them to realize their own potential,
and go after their dreams.
I would teach them to honour, value, to respect themselves,
and tell them not to be mean.
I would teach them to live, love, and laugh
with great joy and simple abundance.

I would be an awesome mentor
I would be someone they can look up to.
I would be like a friend at times.
I would be an authority figure at times.
I want to be someone they can go to if they're in trouble,
if they need someone to talk to.

I would be a fantastic nurse. I would be a healer.
I would try to fix all their cuts and scrapes.
When I can, I would try to fix their mistakes.
If I was a nurse to my children I would want to be there for them
always when I am needed, and never leave them ever.

I would be a great hero.

Margaret Santos

*Hopefully, at some point in my children's lives
I will have been their hero.
To them, I will always be the one they can go to if they need help or
if they need a shoulder to cry on.
The little ones to whom they belong.
The one to whom they can turn to.*

*If I were a mother.....
I would be someone who loves them unconditionally.
I would be an excellent teacher.
I wouldn't tell them what to do,
I'd help them to learn.*

*I would be a counsellor
I would listen and offer support when needed.
I would be a mentor.
I'd be like their best friend, someone to turn to
when they need a helping hand.
I would be a nurse
It would be important because I would try to heal them
physically, emotionally, and spiritually.
I would be a hero.
I would be the one to whom they can always count on.
If I were a mother...*

The Story Behind If I Were a Mother. . .

These are all the things I wished I would have been had I been a mother. I would have been a great teacher who taught my children right from wrong and to be kind, caring, and intelligent people who are strong. I would help them with their homework and teach them that it pays to do hard work, but then I would teach them how to relax and have a little time to play.

If I were a mother, I would be a good counsellor; I would offer my children guidance and teach them to recognize their potential and follow their dreams. I would teach my children to honour, value, and respect themselves and never to be mean. I would teach them to live, laugh, and love with great joy and simple abundance.

I would be an awesome mentor, someone my children could look up to every now and again and someone they could turn to if they were in trouble or needed to talk. I'd be a friend to them and an authoritative figure. All these things I'd be if I were a mother.

Had I been a mother, I would be a fantastic nurse, a healer who would tend to all their cuts and scrapes and fix all their mistakes. I would've been a fantastic nurse if I had been a mother.

If I had children, I would be their hero to whom they could run to for help or a shoulder to cry on. I would love them unconditionally and offer them compassion, understanding, and patience.

That's what I missed most when growing up with my mother, and that's why I would try to be all of those things to my children if I had any of my own, but sadly I did not have any, so I just do it through my writing.

Here's To the World's #1 Dad

Here`s to the world's greatest Dad
Thank you for teaching me to be a lady
Thank you for teaching me to be a gentleman
Thank you for teaching me right from wrong
Thank you for teaching me to be strong

Thank you for teaching me how to be courageous and brave
Thank you for teaching me to fight with my words and not with my
fists
Thank you for teaching me to dispel any of those unwanted myths
Thank you for teaching me more importantly how to pick my battles
and knowing when to walk away

Thank you for teaching me it`s okay to be sensitive
Thank you for teaching me not to be so competitive
Thank you for teaching me it is alright to ask questions
Thank you for teaching me it`s alright to make suggestions
Thank you for teaching me it`s alright to stand up for
what you believe in

Thank you for teaching me it`s not alright to aggravate people
Thank you for teaching me acceptance
Thank you for teaching me tolerance
Thank you for teaching me how to remain calm.
Thank you for teaching me how to live my life with
dignity and integrity
Thank you for teaching me how to be loyal and to live
my life with humility

Thank you for lending me financial support when I needed it the
most
Thank you for always teaching me to be myself

Blooms

Thank you for teaching me to love myself
Thank you for teaching me to look with my eyes
and listen with my heart
Thank you for helping me to make a brand-new start.

35

The Story Behind Here's To the World`s #1 Dad

"Here's to the World's #1 Dad" is about all of the things I wish my dad had done for me or the way he had treated me. For example, I wish my father had loved me unconditionally, I wish he had treated me with loving-kindness, compassion, empathy, like I had been intelligent as well as to be humble. As it always felt to me like I was just another pretty face to him, even though I was trying to teach him how to read and write in English. (He was an immigrant from Portugal).

My father was not a good one, and he never really taught me to be self-sufficient, or to be like my brother, and I also witnessed him being abusive towards my mother. To me I think he taught me the type of person that I didn't want to be. He also taught me the type of man that I did not want in my life. I think both my mother and father taught me the type of individual I want to be by all the interactions they had with each other.

My father didn't teach me how to love myself, nor did he teach me how to live with integrity or to think of myself less. My father, nor my grandfather taught me tolerance if anything they taught me homophobia, but that wasn't something I was interested in being so, I rejected that way of thinking entirely and eventually started accepting all people from all walks of life. In hindsight I don't think there was one good thing my father did aside from having me.

What is love?

Love is special,
Love can be a feeling or an action,
It can also be quite social.
Love is an intense feeling of deep affection.
Love is patient and kind.
Love knows no boundaries.
Love can give a person peace of mind.

Love can feel very lovely.
Loving someone can quite often be misunderstood.
Love always perseveres.
It is not envious of others nor is it proud.
Love can also give you a kick in the derriere
Love should never cause a person to have great strife.
Love should always be an extension of oneself and
an expression of one's life.

Love can be passionate.
But a person should never fear love.
Love can also get quite stale and stagnate.
Because love is a precious gift sent from heaven up above.
Love should always be about trust.
And never about fear or doubt.
It should never be about infatuation and lust.
This type of love you cannot live without.

It never keeps records of any wrong doings.
Love is always very sweet.
It's all about those warm and fuzzy feelings.
Like a delicious peach you pick from a tree, and you eat.
It is all about unconditional love.
That which is sent from God up above.

The Story Behind What is love?

Hopefully, this poem, "What is love?" will teach others a thing or two about love. Love is defined as a strong liking or affection for someone else. Love is vulnerability expressed in the best possible way. Love is patient and kind or it should be anyways. Love is not jealous or boastful. Love can be challenging for some of us, but it should always be about trust. Love should never be about fear or doubt, but sometimes as men and women, we tend to feel insecure about saying that four-letter word.

There are all different kinds of love too! There's love that is expressed between parent and child; there is love that is communicated between two friends; there is romantic love that anyone can express. There are siblings that can express love towards one another, which can be quite nice as well! There is also the love of oneself, and there is compassionate love, too! Spiritual love can be expressed to one's God, or whatever you believe in.

Some people may fear love, but one should never ever, ever, fear love. Love is a risk but if you risk nothing, then you are not living. Love involves putting yourself out there, and yes, love involves being vulnerable, but you know what if you are not vulnerable or putting yourself out there, then you're just not living, and that's not a life I would want.

Beauty Is All Around

Beauty is all around us.
All you have to do is look for it.
You don't have to make a fuss.
What you might like to do is watch, wait, and sit?
People watching can be lots of fun.
You might like to go the park and watch children play.
While you are watching the setting of the sun.
Beauty can be found in all sorts of interesting places such as,
the church where one can go to pray.
Beauty can be found in the most ordinary and simplest of places.
For example, I might find beauty on the face of a child
who is smiling at me.
And it can also be found in small, tight, and enclosed spaces.
Others may find it in a small puppy who gets really excited and
happy.
Wherever, you find it, count yourself as blessed.
Close your eyes, sweet dreams, and go to bed

The Story Behind Beauty Is All Around

Beauty is all around is all about how one can find beauty in the smallest ways. We could find beauty in a child laughing or in a puppy who was guilty of doing something naughty. This poem could be read to a small child who was getting ready for bed. You can watch the sun rising or the setting of the sun which might give you a sense of joy. One might even find beauty in the snow falling, or in children playing in the snow, making snow angels and building snow forts and snowmen. Beauty can be found in the most ordinary of places, in a song on the radio, someone who's singing along, and having a grand old time while doing it. As well as someone whose dancing while no one's watching.

One might find beauty in a child's smile. Beauty can be found in the most ordinary of places: for example, it might be found in two children laughing or playing a board game. It may even be found in two people who are truly and deeply in love and they're getting married, that might bring a smile to your face, and that is where real beauty can be found.

To The Perfect Friend

Here's to my good friend Lorraine,
Who is the perfect friend
Who will probably remain
With me 'til the bitter end
In my heart, never to be a part for too long
As she will always be my bestest ever friend.
She is probably the most optimistic and happiest person I know
She doesn't like to put on a show
She is incredibly humble
Lorraine is quite a person, even remarkable
You might say,
Lorraine is the perfect friend
She is always singing or humming a merry little tune
She is one of the kindest and sweetest people I have ever met
She never settles
She will never judge
Nor will she budge
On any of her principles
And so, she shouldn't
She's probably one of the strongest people I know too.
She has overcome so much in her life
She has beaten cancer not once but twice,
She has overcome a stroke and bleeding on the brain
But she will not let that slow her down
You won't see her frown.
Lorraine is the perfect friend.
Now she does have problems with her speech.
As well as, mobility issues but she can still walk with the
use of her cane

*And she could still get around the Village in her
manual wheelchair
Using one of her arms and one of her legs
I believe it's the left half of her body that still works properly,
if I am not mistaken
She has got all of her favourite Disney movies in her room.
And she is one of the happiest people I know.
And I truly love my dear, sweet friend Lorraine.
I love her to the moon and back again.
I'm afraid that will never ever change.
As she is beautiful from the inside out.
She is so sweet, kind, and compassionate.
I really do not know what I would do without her happy
presence in my life.
She is really the one and only person in my life who doesn't
cause me too much strife.
My perfect friend, Lorraine Coffin.
She also lives with Type I Diabetes, I believe.
I think with time brings opportunities for great change.
She is much more flexible than she used to be.
You will never see her sad, Or mad,
At least for not too long anyways.
That's one of the reasons I'll say "Hello sunshine," to her all the time.
As it'll make me feel better and others too!
She's not one to hold a grudge.
And don't you worry,
if you're looking for your perfect friend,
Be patient and kind with yourself, and give it time.
He or she is out there somewhere
All you have to do is keep looking,
And when you find that special someone,
It'll surely make you smile,
For you have just found the one and only your perfect and forever
friend.
The perfect friend from now until all of eternity.
My best friend for now, and until the day I die, Ms. Lorraine Coffin.*

The Story Behind To The Perfect Friend

"To My Perfect Friend" is about how this wonderful young sixty-seven-year-old Lorraine Ellen Coffin has become one of the most important people in my life. I just want to let her, and everybody know that, especially while she is still with us in this world.

I also want to let everyone know why she is the perfect friend. She is the perfect friend because she will not judge you. She is among the sweetest, kindest, humblest people I have ever met. She is compassionate. She is never sad or mad for too long and does not hold a grudge. She is the happiest, most optimistic person I know. She also doesn't let anything worry her. She is not the most patient person and can get easily get frustrated. However, she is the sweetest, cutest, loving, and lovable person I know.

Lorraine is a remarkably strong, brave, and courageous woman. She has had two types of cancers and lives with type 1 diabetes, yet she does all this with a smile and never a complaint can be heard from her lips. Nope! She can be heard humming a happy little tune in her room, wheeling down the hallway and in her bathroom, of all places, but everyone knows the acoustics are good in the bathroom.

She has got the best laugh too, especially if you can make her laugh from her belly. That is the best, and it doesn't take much for that to happen; all you have to do is say something silly, and she will be laughing out loud.

The purpose of this poem is to tell the reader just how important it is to have someone like Lorraine in my life; someone who is intelligent, kind, giving, doesn't mind sharing, is compassionate, forgiving, humble, reliable, responsible, dependable, but most importantly, loves me for who I am no matter what my flaws or weaknesses. She loves me unconditionally without no reservations. That is why she is my perfect friend.

She makes me feel so good about myself. I don't have to be in the same room as her; I just think of her and feel better.

I was sick one Christmas, and she gave me the nicest present; tea and some chocolates. I wasn't expecting anything from her, and that was such a huge surprise that I started to cry, but they were tears of joy, not sadness.

Lorraine is happy all the time, and that makes me happy too. I wasn't always happy, but now I am. My good friend Lorraine Coffin has also taught me to be grateful for what I have and to look at my cup as half full rather than half empty. But the most important lesson she has taught me is how to be a better version of myself.

I'm Not Just Another Pretty Face

I'm not just another pretty face.
I am a human being, with an excellent mind.
I'm a citizen of this country,
With lots of potential and possibility
For the opportunity for growth and learning
I am a person with a great deal of patience and understanding.
I am a woman who has the capacity to love very deeply and
with great passion.
I am also very mature.
Also, happen to be a lover of nature.
Yes, it's true I am part Portuguese and Jamaican.
And that is where my external beauty comes from
But I'm not just another pretty face.
In this world, I need to find my place.
I am a humanitarian.
There is so much more to me than just looks.
I used to love to read books.

I am intelligent and kind.
I've got a really sharp mind.
I've got a great sense of humour.
I am truly one of a kind.
I can almost compare myself to a flower.
I am beautiful from the inside out.
I am like an onion where you've got to peel back the layers before you
can get to the core.
And that's where the real beauty is hidden.
Deep, deep in the centre of a person's heart,
For that is the truly remarkable part.

Margaret Santos

I am determined and also very dependable.
I am an extremely loyal friend,
And I would stay with you until the bitter end.

The Story Behind I'm Not Just Another Pretty Face

"I'm not just another pretty face" is about how I used to feel about how others viewed me. Not that I think I am so incredibly attractive, but I do believe that I am cute. I just don't think that is my only attribute.

There is so much more to me than my beauty. There's my intelligence, my compassionate and loving heart. I am a woman, a survivor of childhood trauma, and a citizen of this country. I'm very mature for my age, probably because I was diagnosed with this rare condition, Morquio Syndrome B, when I was eight. I am missing the gene to break down these long chains of sugar molecules. This condition mainly affects my joints and my movements, and it also affects my speech. Oh, and I also have rheumatoid arthritis.

I'm also very determined, intelligent, patient, and understanding. I have this great capacity to love. I am also very thoughtful and generous. In my lifetime, I have been a student at Sheridan College; I have been a daughter, a sister, a cousin, a volunteer, a humanitarian of many different causes, including food drives, pennies for water, and shoe boxes for abused women. I've done Socks 4 Souls, raised money for Hands Up 4 Haiti, and quite recently, helped raise money for those in war-torn Ukraine. I am also a published author of many poems and short stories in books with The Poetry Institute of Canada. My very first children's book, available on Amazon, is entitled *An Attitude of Gratitude*.

So, you see, I am much more than just another pretty face.

Margaret Santos

Pride

I am proud to be Canadian.
I am proud to be a woman.
I am proud that I am living with a disability;
However, at times how unpleasant that may be?
I wouldn't have it any other way.
I am proud that I am now comfortable with myself
I am proud that I can put some of my troubles on the top shelf
out of my reach.
I just take things as they are and take it day by day.
I am proud that I am not racist nor am I prejudiced.
I am proud that I am still open-minded.
I am proud to be the confident, beautiful, intelligent, young
woman I have become despite my abusive past.
I am proud that I am a survivor.
I am proud because I have graduated from high school &
Sheridan College.
I am proud because I am still mobile and am still able to
get out and about,
And talking with the use of my communication device.
I am proud as I am beautiful from the inside out.
I am proud because I am a research champion.
I am proud that I sit on the Village Advisory Team.
I am proud that I am not cross or mean.

I am proud because I have travelled to Edmonton, Alberta as a Walk
With Me Ambassador, and learned a lot.
I am proud because I am a published author.
I am proud because I am very strong.
I am proud because I still try to be as independent as I can be.

Blooms

I am proud because I am still a very determined individual.
I am proud to be so comfortable with myself at this point and time in my
life that I make decisions for myself and know that they
are the right ones.
I a proud that I am still able to laugh and have fun.
I am proud that I can be myself authentically.
I am proud that I love myself unconditionally.
I am proud that I am able to recognize all my abilities.
I am proud that I am still able to recognize all of my weaknesses &
insecurities.
I am proud that I do inspire.
I am proud that I wasn't brought up to be a thief or a liar.
I am proud that I feel comfortable enough to show myself entirely.
I am proud that I am brave enough to be real.
I am proud that I am comfortable with my sexuality.
I am proud that I am honest and trustworthy.
I am also very sorry.
For those living in Orlando, and those victims who were shot
at Pulse Night Club.

It is such a tragedy for something you obviously cannot change,
But just remember love is a gift sent from God up above.
Spread the love all around.
Right from the ground up to the sky.
All we can do is try.

The Story Behind Pride

This poem is a reflection on the many things I am proud of. I am proud of my accomplishments, who I am, and what I value as a woman and a person. I appreciate how physically strong I am, brave and courageous, and proud that I am still here. As a child, I was abused sexually, physically, emotionally, and even financially, but I am proud of the wonderful young woman I have grown into.

I am proud of my intelligence; I am proud of the fact that I have recently discovered my loving, caring, more compassionate self. I am also so proud of the many obstacles I have had to overcome due to the trauma I have suffered at the hands of my family members and some of my peers from school, and also my disability that I live with every day.

I have had to overcome learning to walk again after having a bilateral hip transplant, and for those of you who don't know what that is, it's having both of your hips replaced one right after the other. I have also had partial shoulder replacement surgery.

I had to relearn to walk with the use of a walker. That was no easy feat.

I am super-duper proud to be Margret Santos living in the 21st century, and being the person into which I have grown. I am genuinely happy about all my accomplishments and eager to share my gifts with this big, beautiful world.

I am so proud of my resilient spirit. I am also proud of all the work I have done on myself and all the work I continue to do to improve and become a better human being.

To the Queen

Queen Elizabeth the 2nd, passed away peacefully
at Balmoral Castle on Thursday September 8th, 2022.
She was the Greatest of all time
Upon news of her death there were many all over the world
and in the UK crying boo hoo.
And then there was that smile,
She was giving, caring, and selfless
She was an amazing inspiration to us all.
She was not egotistical, boastful, or selfish
Then God came on her to call
And He called her home to be with her King
It was definitely a life well lived
For the people in the streets will rejoice and sing
And a Queen who was very much loved.
A history she was a part
She will now and always be in our heart.

The Story Behind To the Queen

"To the Queen" pays tribute to the late Queen Elizabeth II and her seventy-year reign as the head of state of the United Kingdom. She was a phenomenal woman who served in WWII and a tiny woman with a huge personality.

Her Royal Highness Queen Elizabeth II was a serious, no-nonsense woman. She was also a very optimistic woman with a cheery disposition who always looked for the best in people. She was fearless, courageous, and stoic; if she was upset or bothered by something, one would not know it. She was also very humble and gracious, always putting duty first ahead of her needs. In other words, she always put the thoughts and feelings of others ahead of her own feelings.

She was a wife to her husband, Prince Philip, the Duke of Edinburgh, for seventy-four years, until his passing in April of 2021. She was a devoted mother to her four children, a dedicated grandmother to her six grandchildren, and a loving great-grandmother to her eight great-grandchildren.

She was a classy lady with an open and giving heart; she conducted herself with dignity and integrity. She tried to include everyone, not excluding anyone, so no one would feel left out. She acted with such an heir for how everyone else was feeling by putting herself in the shoes of those she served. She was one of those people who was kind, caring, giving and compassionate. She was a guide and an example to us all of how one could give to others and be completely selfless while still being able to take care of oneself.

Rest well, your Royal Highness Queen Elizabeth II.

Metamorphosis

As in the life cycle of a butterfly
I was quite shy.
Restless, reserved, and quiet; I was in a world of my own
Like a butterfly, I started off in a cocoon
To emerge from it not too, too soon.

I was not very confident
In fact, I myself was quite insecure
And unsure all together.
I took French, English, and Drama all throughout high school.
Which you would think might actually build my self-confidence.

From numerous counsellors I sought lots of guidance.
I grew up to develop my intelligence.
Making numerous mistakes along the way;

However, taking it day by day.
Soon I would not make the same mistakes over and over again.

Lots of clothes, I bought.
To help me feel better,
In other words, look good on the outside
Later on, work on the inside,
But that did not work out for me either.

I was used, and my body was abused
But just you look at me now.
When you see me passing you need not frown.
You should feel inspired.
And I am saying that with the utmost integrity.

Eventually, I came out of that shell I had built for myself
all these years.
I took yoga, and I started to take up art which eventually

opened up my heart.
I also started to write again, and began to do gardening.
I used to be someone who could easily be conformed to another idea;

However, I observed, and listened with my ears.
Ultimately, to be transformed.
From this small, timid, and reserved person.
To this passionate and very phenomenal young woman.
Like the butterfly.
I have been completely transformed.
This is called metamorphosis,
That is what this is.
I have learned to give my all
Without expecting anything in return.
That is a good way to learn.

It is also a good way to teach yourself
How to be kind,
And to keep a firm hold on your peace of mind.
To treat others with dignity and respect.
It also gives you a chance to reflect.

It gives a person a chance to work on his or her intellectual abilities.
It also gives them the chance to develop a good sense of ones own
necessities

And what is important to them?
It is a good way to learn to be selfless.
It is a good way of not becoming relentless.

Like the butterfly,

I have been transformed
To again be reborn
From my cocoon I emerged
A changed person.
Just like the butterfly.
I came from a different place

As you can plainly see by the expression on my face.
I am happy now. Fully and completely.

The Story Behind Metamorphosis

The poem, "Metamorphosis"is about my transformation from a shy, insecure teenager to the phenomenal young woman I am today. It's about how I felt so small, timid, and unsure of myself. It's about all the things I have done to feel better about myself between that time and now and all of the crap I've had to put up with between my family and my peers from school. It's about overcoming all my challenges and everything between that time and now. It's about all I have endured, from the abuse when I was a young child to how my body was abused into early adulthood. It's about all the lessons I have learned and what I've taken away from them. Essentially, it's about the journey, not about the destination. It's about a person who felt absolutely worthless and me finally beginning to understand my worth and purpose as a human being living on this earth.

I aim to live as full a life as possible despite all my limitations. My purpose is to give as much as possible with all my strengths and weaknesses. My goal is to give as much of my heart as is humanly possible. My purpose is to educate people as well as entertain them. The purpose of my being here is to find out who I really and truly am and to get about the business of making as many connections as possible.

So, as one might find it hard to believe, I have had to build up these invisible brick walls around me to protect and keep me safe. I no longer need these invisible walls which have kept me secure all these years. I have now shed my protective wall, and I am free to be authentic and show all of me - the real true me.

Acknowlededgment

I would like to express my heartfelt gratitude to my publisher, Pricely Francis, my Chaplain and President of Vase On Table Publishing . His support and dedication throughout the entire publishing process was unwavering. Without his expertise, guidance, and commitment to excellence, bringing my work to life would not have been possible.

Pricely encouraged me to publish my poems. He was a constant source of inspiration and motivation and invested countless hours reviewing and editing my manuscript. I am also indebted to him for his cover design work.

I would also like to acknowledge the publisher's unwavering belief in my voice as an author and a poet. His unwavering support and faith in my creative endeavors have given me the confidence to pursue my passion and share my stories with the world.

To my publisher, Chaplain and Spiritual Guide, thank you for your invaluable partnership, professionalism, and dedication. Your contribution to this book's success is immeasurable, and I am truly grateful for your reliable guidance and support.

About The Author

Margaret Nembhard Santos lives in Canada, Mississauga, Ontario. She is a resident at The Village of Erin Meadows long term care home run by Schlegel Villages since 2002.

Margaret is actively involved in the life of the Village despite suffering from rheumatoid arthritis and a rare condition, "Morquio Syndrome B" in which the gene that breaks down long-chain sugar molecules is missing. The disease has several manifestations but mainly affects her joints, mobility and speech.

She studied General Arts and Sciences (.G.A.S.) at Sheridan College. She graduated with a one-year certificate as a part of her Post-Secondary education. Margaret also did the Social Service Worker program at the same College, but was unable to complete the course due to health challenges.

Margaret writes for Erin Meadows' newsletter, *The Villager* and has published many other Anthologies with The Poetry Institute of Canada. She has published works in twelve of their books, some of which are *Island Magic, Mists of Morning, The Tracery of Trees, Springs Gentle Rain.* She is of a children's book, *An Attitude of Gratitude.*

She has an Award of Excellence for her short story entitled "In Her Honour." She likes to paint, read, and write in her spare time. She also spearheads food drives and any other causes that improve living conditions in the community.